Go Ahead, Start that Business! Quick Guide for Starting Your Own Business

By Dr. Nicole L. Ross, Ph.D.

I0492610

© November 2020
www.newpcs.org

Table of Contents:

📎 **Do Your Research**

📎 **Business Plan**

📎 **Business Funding**

📎 **Open A Business Bank Account**

📎 **Business Structures**

📎 **Get Registered**

📎 **Purchase Your Domain**

📎 **Website Creation**

📎 **Marketing + Advertising**

📎 **Create a Schedule**

📎 **Know Your Worth**

Starting a business involves planning, making key financial decisions, and completing a series of legal activities. This book is designed to help you understand this process. If you have ever wanted to have your own business but did not know where to start or what to do, this book is for you. It covers all essential start-up tips needed to turn that witty idea into a flourishing business. Now, let's get started!

First things first…

<u>DO YOUR RESEARCH</u>

Market research will tell you if there is an opportunity to turn your idea into a successful business. It is a way to gather information about potential customers shopping patterns; their likes and dislikes. Market research is also a way to know what other businesses are already operating in your area and their successes and failures.

When conducting market research, a SWOT Analysis is often used. SWOT Analysis is a simple but useful framework for analyzing your organization's strengths, weaknesses, opportunities, and threats of the current market you are trying to enter. It helps you to build on what you do well, to address what you're lacking, to minimize risks, and to take the greatest possible advantage of chances for success. Use the information you obtain in your SWOT Analysis to establish a competitive advantage for your business. Then implement that into a successful business plan.

BUSINESS PLAN

A Business Plan has two primary purposes. First and foremost, it should be used to help run your company with a more cohesive vision. It is your roadmap. By truly analyzing your plan for marketing, sales, manufacturing, website design, etc., you greatly improve your chances for success. Your business plan is the foundation of your business. It is a roadmap for how to structure, run, and grow your new business. Consider your business plan as the blueprint for your business.

The second purpose of a Business Plan is that a financial institution or other lender will not invest in your company unless you can demonstrate that you have a roadmap to success. Banks want to mitigate their risk of default, and private investors, such as angel investors, want a realistic forecast for when they will be reaping a return on their capital.

Simply put, investors and banks want to see that you actually have a plan, and you have already invested in your own company by doing the necessary research to get started. Business plans are used to convince people that working with you or investing in your company is a smart choice. One key thing to remember; however, while having a business plan is an essential part of starting a business, do not let not having one stop you from moving forward and getting started. I have had several clients who have an extremely successful start and come back to get help with a business plan when they are ready to take their business to the next level and secure funding. This leads to the next step in the process of starting a business…funding.

BUSINESS FUNDING

It costs money to start a business. Funding your business is one of the first and most important financial decisions you make as a business owner. When starting a business, one of the most challenging obstacles to overcome is getting business funding. Most loans are not available for small businesses until you can provide documentation showing that you have been in business for at least 2-3 years consecutively. There are only a few other options for obtaining business funding, such as using personal funds, business investors, crowdfunding, or Kickstarter.

How you choose to fund your business could affect how you structure and run your business. Using personal funds, otherwise known as bootstrapping, allows you to leverage your own financial resources to support your business. Self-funding can come in the form of turning to family and friends for capital, using your savings accounts, or even tapping into your 401k.

The benefit of using your own funds to start your business is that you retain complete control over the business. On the flip side, you also take on all the risk by yourself. Be careful not to spend more than you can afford, and be especially careful if you choose to tap into retirement accounts early. You might face expensive fees or penalties, or damage your ability to retire on time, so you should always consult with your financial advisor first.

Crowdfunding raises funds for a business from a large number of people, called Crowdfunder's. Crowdfunder's are not technically investors because they do not receive any shares of ownership in the business, and they do not expect a financial return on their money.

Instead, Crowdfunder's expect to get a "gift" from your company as thanks for their contribution. That gift is often the product you plan to sell or other special perks, like meeting the business owner or getting their name in the credits. Crowdfunding is also popular because it is very low risk for business owners. Not only do you get to retain full control of your company, but if your plan fails, you are usually under no obligation to repay your Crowdfunder's. Every crowdfunding platform is different, so make sure to read the fine print and understand your full financial and legal obligations.

Whichever direction you move with getting funding for your business, having a rock-solid business plan will help you figure out how much money you will need to start your business.

OPEN A BUSINESS BANK ACCOUNT

Once you have all of the appropriate documentation filed with the state and IRS, you must open a business bank account. Do your research to determine which bank is right for you. My recommendation is always to start by checking where you do your personal banking because you already have a banking relationship there. Also, check with your local credit unions. Credit Unions typically offer really good banking options for small businesses.

Once you open your business account, you want to start using your business account for all business transactions. These transactions include but are not limited to purchasing supplies, mailing fees (stamps, envelopes, P.O. Box, etc.), transportation (vehicle maintenance, gas), website, web hosting, computer hardware/software, phone service, education/training, meals/entertainment, professional fees, etc.

Once you start selling your products or services, you will connect the business account to your accounting software and have any funds you make deposited directly into your business bank account. In the beginning, you may have to invest your own money into the business bank account, but having the business account will:

(1)   Help you maintain a budget for the business

(2)   Help you track all of your expenses for the business

(3)   Makes it easier to provide documentation at the end of the year when preparing for taxes such as expense reports, profit and loss statements, and balance sheets.

Dun & Bradstreet D-U-N-S Number

After all, the appropriate paperwork has been filed with the state and IRS, apply for a Dun & Bradstreet D-U-N-S number. The Dun & Bradstreet D-U-N-S Number is a unique nine-digit identifier for businesses. Having this number will help you establish your business credit.

A simple way to build business credit is to create a net-30 business account with companies like Uline or Quill in your business name. A net-30 account is one that gives you 30 days to pay your bill in full after you have purchased products. A net-30 account is a vendor credit that allows you to buy now and pay later. Net-30 vendors that report those payments to commercial credit agencies help your company establish a strong business credit history.

A hint of caution, however, this process may take a while. After you have had your net-30 accounts for some time, the next step is to look into getting a business gas card. After the gas card, eventually, try and get a business credit card. When applying for a business credit card, search to see who is offering the best incentives. A good start is by reaching out to where you already have your business bank account. Again, it may seem like a slow or tedious process, but the goal is to eventually get to a place where you do not have to invest your own money continuously, and the business will sustain itself.

BUSINESS STRUCTURES

The legal structure you choose for your business will impact your business registration requirements, how much you pay in taxes, and your personal liability. This structure influences everything from day-to-day operations, taxes, and how much of your personal assets are at risk. It is imperative to choose a business structure that gives you the right balance of legal protections and benefits.

In the beginning phases of business development, it is always good to speak with a certified tax professional about the type of business structure best for your business. You will need to choose a business structure before you register the business with the state or register to get an employer identification number and file for the appropriate licenses and permits.

Next, you will find a very brief description of the different business structures. Please do your research when deciding the structure of your business. This is an important decision. Choose wisely.

Sole Proprietorship

A sole proprietorship gives you complete control of your business. You are automatically considered a sole proprietorship if you do business activities but do not register as any other business type.

Sole proprietorships do not produce a separate business entity. This means that your business assets and liabilities are not separate from your personal assets and liabilities. You can be held personally liable for the debts and obligations of the business. It can also be hard to get funding because banks are hesitant to lend to sole proprietorships.

Partnership

Partnerships are the simplest structure for two or more people to own a business together. There are two common partnerships: limited partnerships (LP) and limited liability partnerships (LLP).

Limited partnerships have only one general partner with unlimited liability, and all other partners have limited liability. The partners with limited liability also tend to have limited control over the company, which is documented in a partnership agreement. Limited liability partnerships are similar to limited partnerships but give limited liability to every owner. An LLP protects each partner from debts against the partnership; they will not be responsible for other partners' actions.

Limited Liability Company (LLC)

An LLC lets you take advantage of the benefits of both the corporation and partnership business structures. LLCs protect you from personal liability. In most instances, your personal assets like your vehicle, house, and savings accounts will not be at risk if your LLC faces bankruptcy or lawsuits. Profits and losses can get passed through to your personal income without facing corporate taxes. However, LLC members are considered self-employed and must pay self-employment tax contributions towards Medicare and Social Security.

The following are the list of filing fees for each state for a
Limited Liability Company (LLC):

Alabama $163	Hawaii $50	Massachusetts $500	New Mexico $50	South Dakota $150
Alaska $250	Idaho $100	Michigan $50	New York $200	Tennessee $300
Arizona $50	Illinois $150	Minnesota $155	North Carolina $125	Texas $300
Arkansas $45	Indiana $95	Mississippi $50	North Dakota $135	Utah $70
California $70	Iowa $50	Missouri $50	Ohio $99	Vermont $125
Colorado $50	Kansas $160	Montana $70	Oklahoma $100	Virginia $100
Connecticut $120	Kentucky $40	Nebraska $105	Oregon $100	Washington $200
Delaware $90	Louisiana $100	Nevada $425	Pennsylvania $125	West Virginia $100
Florida $125	Maine $175	New Hampshire $100	Rhode Island $150	Wisconsin $130
Georgia $100	Maryland $100	New Jersey $125	South Carolina $110	Wyoming $100

*These fees are subject to change

Corporations

C-Corp (Corporation)

A corporation, sometimes called a C-Corp, is a legal entity that is separate from its owners. Corporations can make a profit, be taxed, and can be held legally liable.

Corporations offer the strongest protection to owners from personal liability, but the cost to form a corporation is higher than other structures. Corporations also require more extensive record-keeping, operational processes, and reporting. Unlike sole proprietors, partnerships, and LLCs, corporations pay income tax on their profits. In some cases, corporate profits are taxed twice; first, when the company makes a profit, and again when dividends are paid to shareholders on their personal tax returns.

S-Corp (S-Corporation)

An S corporation, sometimes called an S-Corp, is a special type of corporation designed to avoid the double taxation drawback of regular C-Corps. S-Corps allow profits, and some losses, to be passed through directly to owners personal income without ever being subject to corporate tax rates.

S-Corps must file with the IRS to get S-Corp status, a different process from registering with your state. S-Corps also have an independent life, just like C corps. If a shareholder leaves the company or sells their shares, the S-Corp can continue doing business relatively undisturbed.

B-Corp (Benefit Corporation)

A benefit corporation, sometimes called a B-Corp, is a for-profit corporation recognized by a majority of the United States. B-Corps are different from C-Corps in purpose, accountability, and transparency, but are not different in how they are taxed. There are several third-party B-Corp certification services, but none are required for a company to be legally considered a B-Corp in a state where the legal status is available.

Close Corporation

Close corporations resemble B-Corps but have a less traditional corporate structure. State rules vary, but shares are usually barred from public trading. A small group of shareholders can run close corporations without a board of directors.

Non-profit Corporation

Non-profit corporations are organized to do charity, education, religious, literary, or scientific work. Because their work benefits the public, nonprofits can receive tax-exempt status, meaning they do not pay state or federal income taxes on any profits it makes.

Non-profits must file with the IRS to get tax exemption, a different process from registering with the state. Non-profits are often called 501(c)(3) corporations, a reference to the Internal Revenue Code section that is most commonly used to grant tax-exempt status.

Cooperative

A cooperative is a business or organization owned by and operated to benefit those using its services. Profits and earnings generated by the cooperative are distributed among the members, also known as user-owners. Typically, an elected board of directors and officers run the cooperative, while regular members have voting power to control the direction of the cooperative. Members can become part of the cooperative by purchasing shares, though the amount of shares they hold does not affect the weight of their vote.

GET REGISTERED

To take your business from an idea to an actual entity, you have to legitimize it and register with the state. This step is done after you have identified your business structure. Once you determine the structure and you are ready to file with the state, (1) check to see if the name is available by doing a Business Entity Search (2) triple check to make sure your application is filled out correctly and all information is accurate. Once your business is registered, check to see if there are any insurance or certification requirements to operate.

Employer Identification Number (EIN)

After filing with the state, the next step is to get an Employer Identification Number (EIN). Your EIN is equivalent to your social security number; only it is for your business. An Employer Identification Number (EIN) is also known as a federal tax identification number, and is used to identify a business entity. An employer identification number (EIN) is a nine-digit number assigned by the IRS. It is used to identify the tax accounts of employers and certain others who have no employees. The IRS uses the number to identify taxpayers who are required to file various business tax returns. I strongly encourage you to obtain your EIN immediately after filing with the state. Obtaining an EIN is **FREE** with the IRS. You can do so by visiting the IRS website directly. Do not pay anyone for an EIN!

Depending on the entity type you decide and business activities, you may need to set up a Sales and Use tax account. This is not something you will do until you have your first product or contract and are ready to sell and start making money. For more information about any taxes you have to pay, contact the state Department of Revenue where your business is registered and/or a certified public accountant.

PURCHASE YOUR DOMAIN

Now that all the required paperwork is filed, you are officially ready to do business. Before you make that first sale, you have to purchase your domain. Do this even if you are not prepared to build your website. Buy your domain, so you have it when you are ready. There are several options for where to purchase a domain.

Do some research and see where you can find the domain you want for the best price. As a rule of thumb when selecting a domain, the domain name should be easy to remember and as simple as possible. Why? Because it will be on all of your marketing material, and you do not want to be stuck with a long domain that is difficult to fit on business cards or flyers.

WEBSITE CREATION

Once your domain is purchased and you are ready to go to the next phase of your business, it is time to design your website. When building the website, think about your ideal client. Put yourself in your client's shoes when creating the site. You want to make sure you are targeting them in the website design. Branding is essential. You want to have a unified look and feel of your entire brand across all platforms. Your website should not be a total 360 from your logo or social media platforms. The brand needs to be consistent across the board.

I have had a few people ask if they even need a website, and my response to this is always YES! Absolutely you need one. No matter if your business provides a product or service, having a website is a must. Why? There are several reasons, but I will just list a few.

(1) A website makes your company appear professional and more credible than companies that only have a social media page.

(2) Having a website is a great way to attract potential new customers through Search Engine Optimization (SEO). When people typically look for the product or service you provide, your company will come up.

(3) Having a website allows you to create the narrative for your company. You can highlight your experience, showcase pictures, and broadcast customer reviews or testimonials.

MARKETING + ADVERTISING

Marketing is the process of identifying customer needs and determining how best to meet those needs. Identifying your target market is pinpointing who you want to buy your service or product.

In contrast, advertising is promoting your company and its products or services through paid channels. Advertisements are what you see on billboards when you drive down the road, hear on the radio, and see in between television shows. Knowing your target market will help you create effective advertisements for your company.

Another way to advertise your company is through social media. There are several social media platforms, and here are a few examples: Facebook, Instagram, Twitter, YouTube, Pinterest, Snapchat, and Tumblr.

<u>Use Social Media Intentionally</u>! Follow people who inspire you and who are doing what you want to do. Look at what they are doing and see how you can implement that into your company. You do not have to reinvent the wheel.

Observe others in your industry and get some ideas. Use social media to promote your business. It would be best if you had a profile on as many social media platforms as possible. You need CONTENT, CONTENT, CONTENT! Make your content is relevant to the products you provide. Incorporate pictures, videos, live feeds, questions, articles, and any other creative ideas to keep your followers engaged and grow your social media.

<u>You Are Your Brand.</u> Consider getting t-shirts/ polos/sweatshirts made to wear to networking and vendor events as well as while you're out taking care of errands. Why advertise

another company's brand, when you have your own?

When people see you, they should see your company. Additional material useful for spreading the word about your business and connecting with new customers is business cards, flyers, brochures, etc. When it comes to social media management there are several options available. You can download post scheduling software to connect all of your social platforms and schedule posts. Utilizing one of these will help you save time, but it is not something you have to do. Many of the social media platforms are already connected. You can also hire an actual social media manager. Again, not something you have to do but it will help you save time throughout your day. Try your best to post to social media at least once a day - put it on your schedule.

CREATE A SCHEDULE

Creating a schedule has to be one of the hardest parts of having your own business. Scheduling is the art of planning your activities so that you can achieve your goals and priorities in the time you have available. You must develop a set schedule and stick to it as much as possible. Time is the one resource that we cannot buy, but we often waste it or use it ineffectively. You are only one person, so scheduling your time is more important than you may realize, especially when you have various other obligations that require time. Scheduling helps you think about what you want to achieve in a day, week, or month, and it keeps you on track to accomplish your goals. When scheduling is done effectively, it helps you:

- Make sure you have enough time for essential tasks.

- Avoid taking on more than you can handle.

- Understand what you can realistically achieve with your time.

- Add contingency time for "the unexpected."

- Achieve a good work-life balance.

My recommendation is to delegate a time block every day; for example, 9am-10am: Posting on Social Media 10am-11am: Shopping for supplies, etc. Everything you do requires time; making your products, checking/responding to emails, answering/returning phone calls, posting on social media, working to increase followers, ordering miscellaneous marketing material, etc. Use your time wisely and get it done.

Remember, if you do not do it, it will not get done. Plan accordingly.

<u>KNOW YOUR WORTH</u>

I will keep this short and sweet. Know your worth. One of the most straightforward rules in business ownership is having the ability to truly understand your own value and self-worth, knowing exactly what skills and abilities you bring to the table each day, as well as how valuable this is in comparison to others performing a similar job, will give you an important edge. Knowing your worth is one of the most important things you can do as a business owner. When you know your value, you honor yourself enough to ask for it!

Having a business is like having a baby. You have to nurture it. You have to spend time with it. You have to sacrifice for it. You have to promote it for the world to see.

There are only have 24 hours in a day. It is hard to put a price tag on time, but you must determine how much each of those hours is worth to you as a business owner. Name your price and stick to it. Never sell yourself short.

Believe in the product or service you provide. Entrepreneurship can be very challenging, yet extremely rewarding. It is not for the faint at heart. I believe in you. I believe in your desire not only to be an entrepreneur but leave a lasting legacy of generational wealth for your family.

It has been my pleasure to help give you a *New Perspective* as you contemplate the process of owning a business.

Now, Go Ahead…Start that Business!

***For additional assistance with starting your business or to answer any questions you may have about how to apply the content in this book, please contact Dr. Ross with New Perspective Consulting Services at <u>www.newpcs.org</u> to set up a consultation. ***